IN THE SHADOWS OF HOLY WEEK

The Office of Tenebrae

COMPILED WITH AN INTRODUCTION BY
The Rev. Frederick C. Elwood
Rector, St. John's Episcopal Church
Olympia, Washington

EDITED BY
The Rev. Dr. John L. Hooker
Chapel Musician and
Associate Professor of Music and Pastoral Theology
Episcopal Divinity School
Cambridge, Massachusetts

THE CHURCH HYMNAL CORPORATION, NEW YORK

The Church Hymnal Corporation
445 Fifth Avenue
New York, N.Y. 10016

INTRODUCTION

" *Tenebrae factae sunt, dum crucifixissent Jesum...*

Darkness covered the whole land when Jesus had been crucified . . . "

This is primarily a service booklet or "order of service." Its purpose is to make the ancient Holy Week rite of Tenebrae accessible to parishes of all sizes. It is meant to be an act of worship into which all who attend may enter fully.

Although Tenebrae is not a complicated liturgy, it is also not as familiar as the other Holy Week services. This booklet, therefore, begins with a brief survey of Tenebrae's origin and purpose. The "how to," "when," and "why" concerns that participants may have are also considered.

The liturgy offered in the following pages is the full, ancient form of Tenebrae as it appears in basic outline in *The Book of Occasional Services*.[1] This booklet develops that outline, providing all of the materials necessary for a simple, edifying recitation of the office: All of the psalms, canticles, responsories and readings are reproduced in full and in a size large enough to be read with ease. Worshipers are thus spared the distractions of having to cope with more than one book and with print that is too small. Congregations, moreover, may choose either to sing or to say the psalms and canticles; the format facilitates either method of recitation. For added convenience the appointed antiphons are printed both before and after the psalms and canticles to which they apply; page turning is thus kept to a minimum. Finally, the rubrics guide participants smoothly through each phase of the service.

Tenebrae will, of course, best fulfill its spiritual purpose if the service is introduced well in advance of Holy Week. The history and purpose of Tenebrae might be explained through a series of bulletin inserts during the weeks of Lent. Tenebrae preparations might also be made during adult classes on Sunday mornings or at mid-week Lenten gatherings. One of the two latter options will be especially desirable if the congregation plans to use the musical settings for the psalms and canticles.

---

[1] New York: The Church Hymnal Corporation, 1991, p. 72-90.

Tenebrae is a moving descent into the darkest days of the church year. The office will require preparation. But pastors and worship committees who introduce Tenebrae offer their congregations a most helpful spiritual exercise. The balance of Holy Week will be enhanced by this simple meditation. This is true, in part, because the final three days of the week (traditionally known as the *Triduum sacrum*) have developed in recent years a certain structural integrity, an obvious symmetry. The events of Maundy Thursday, Good Friday and Holy Saturday are now neatly framed by Wednesday's Tenebrae, which descends from the light into darkness, and Saturday's Great Vigil, which ascends out of darkness into the brilliance of the resurrection. On Wednesday evening we enter the shadowy enclosure fashioned by Tenebrae and the Great Vigil. Within it we are witnesses as pride, jealousy and hatred appear to defeat goodness and extinguish hope. Thus our exit from this darkened space on Easter constitutes a glorious new exodus. We experience anew the victory over the powers of darkness that is ours in the Light of Christ.

ORIGINS

The urge to involve greater numbers of people in the church's worship during Holy Week seems over the centuries to have provided incentive for a union of the traditional morning prayer-hours of Matins and Lauds. The merger of these two rites produced an additional office intended for use only during Holy Week. Since the twelfth century this service has been known as Tenebrae.

Scheduling was a key factor in the development of Tenebrae. The church's customary hours of prayer began in the very early hours of the morning. Both Tertullian (c.160–c.225), and Hippolytus (c.170–c.236) urged the faithful to engage in private devotions at prescribed intervals throughout the day. In addition to the usual morning and evening prayers, they recommended meditations at the third, sixth and ninth hours of the day (approximately 9 AM, Noon, and 3 PM), as well as worship and prayer at midnight.[2]

These patterns of devotion appear to have influenced the structured life of communal prayer characteristic of the religious orders of later centuries. In the cloister, as in the early years of Christian devotion, daily prayers began early. St. Benedict's *Rule* (c. 540) for the regulation of monastic life, for example, indicated that Matins, the first office of the day, should begin sometime after midnight and well before dawn. Because the monastic schedule of work, prayer, and study varied according to the season and the liturgical calendar, it is not possible to say with certainty at what hour this office was said. It has, however, been suggested that during the winter months at medieval Monte Cassino, the principal Benedictine monastery, Matins may have begun as early as 2 AM. The next few hours were spent in prayer

---

[2]Josef A. Jungmann, S.J., *The Early Liturgy: To the Time of Gregory the Great*, trans. Francis A. Brunner, C.SS.R., Liturgical Studies, vol. vi (Notre Dame: University of Notre Dame Press, 1959), 100,102.

and reading. Lauds was then said at daybreak.[3] Whatever the schedule may have been precisely, one conclusion seems safe: Even in an age when many people were on their way to work by dawn's light, attendance at these morning offices would have been difficult for most lay men and women. In order to attract worshipers from outside the cloister, some concession to the realities of secular life needed to be made in the Holy Week schedule.

Almost from the beginning of Christian history the week prior to Easter had been a time when daily routines were set aside. By design, Holy Week was meant to be a time "set apart" for immersion in the paschal mystery. The early church had been creative in planning and scheduling services aimed at realizing this goal. In later fourth-century Jerusalem, for example, the intricate structure of Holy Week services described by the pilgrim Egeria had but one goal: The observances were designed to attract and involve people by making our Lord's concluding words and deeds "happen again" in a liturgical present tense. This was accomplished, in part, by linking the final events of Jesus' ministry with the days and approximate hours of their occurrence.[4]

The office of Tenebrae, then, may be viewed as a much later product of the church's longstanding desire to include greater numbers of worshipers in Holy Week's sacred events. Uniting the two early-morning offices of Matins and Lauds into a single liturgy, Tenebrae was said or sung, not in the early hours of the morning, but in the late afternoon or evening of the last three days of Holy Week. Each day had its own particular theme: Thursday's Tenebrae concerned betrayal; Friday's focused upon Jesus' judgment, crucifixion, and death; Christ's burial and the Christian hope of resurrection were the subjects for Saturday. The theme appropriate to each day, however, was transferred to its eve (e.g., the Tenebrae of Good Friday was held on Thursday evening). In this way people outside the monastic community who could not possibly have participated in the early morning hours after midnight were given an opportunity to add these spiritual exercises to their observance of Holy Week.

THE STRUCTURE AND CONTENT OF TENEBRAE

Tenebrae is a Latin word signifying "darkness," "shadows," and "obscurity." It is a word that pointedly calls our attention to the scriptural accounts of our Lord's crucifixion: The name of this service is taken from the opening words of the fifth responsory: *"Tenebrae factae sunt"*—"darkness came over the whole land" (Mark 15:33; also, Matthew 27:45; Luke 23:44). The word *tenebrae* is, therefore, appropriate to both the time and the ceremonies of the

---

[3]David Knowles, *Christian Monasticism*, World University Library (New York: McGraw-Hill Book Company, 1969), 213.

[4]J.G. Davies, ed., *The Westminster Dictionary of Worship* (Philadelphia: The Westminster Press, 1986), s.v. "Holy Week," by A.A. McArthur.

office it identifies. According to a well-ordered liturgical design, Tenebrae's structure works together with its content to evoke the somber mood which will not be dispelled until Holy Week concludes in the Great Vigil of Easter.

Structurally, Tenebrae is characterized by the progressive extinguishing of all lights in the church except one candle. At the liturgy's end the ministers and people depart silently through the shadows cast by this solitary flame.

Complementing and intensifying this liturgical descent into gloom, Tenebrae's content informs and gives substance to the feelings of apprehension stirred by the ebbing light. The appointed psalms, lessons and prayers of Tenebrae form a prolonged contemplation of the events of Jesus' last days, beginning with the Last Supper and ending with his burial. Betrayal, abandonment, judgment, death: these were the terrors through which Jesus moved during his last days. These are the terrors inhabiting the darkness that descends as light fades. And, in the end, these dreadful realities are only slightly relieved by the still obscure hint of resurrection symbolized by the one remaining candle.

MATINS AND LAUDS

The medieval offices of Matins and Lauds which were combined to create Tenebrae were the usual morning offices recited by the monastic communities ministering in the Roman basilicas and collegiate churches of Europe. These liturgies had not yet acquired all of the characteristics of the later Roman (cathedral) offices. Thus, there were no introductory versicles and responses, there was no invitatory, hymns were not included, and the *Gloria Patri* was not said at the end of each psalm.[5]

In Western Christianity Matins (meaning "morning") is the traditional breviary office for the night. At Matins the morning is greeted with prayer even before the sun rises. Matins developed out of the nocturnal times of prayer and watchfulness *(vigiliae)* that were common in the early church. Fostered, in part, by the parable of the wise and foolish maidens (Matthew 25), there was an early and general belief that the *Parousia* (the "Second Coming") would take place at midnight. This expectation may have been responsible for the introduction of the vigils out of which Matins grew. Certainly Jesus' repeated admonitions concerning watchfulness combined with the fate of the foolish, slumbering maidens provided strong incentives to prayerful vigilance in the dead of night.

---

[5]J.G. Davies, ed., *The Westminster Dictionary of Worship* (Philadelphia: The Westminster Press, 1986), s.v. "Tenebrae," by J.D. Crichton.

Although its elements varied according to time and place, Matins traditionally included three distinct sections called Nocturns (meaning "divisions of the night"). In their full and complete form each Nocturn contained three psalms and one extended reading which was divided into three lessons by three responsories.[6] A portion of the book of Lamentations was read during the First Nocturn; patristic readings were offered in the Second; a selection from the New Testament was read during the Third Nocturn. Along with the office itself, this segmentation may have derived from the vigils of the very early church. Vigils were meant to be times of wakefulness when worshipers observed the passage of time through a series of recitations balanced by periods of silence. The well-ordered progression through the three Nocturns provided the devotional rhythm characteristic of a vigil.

The office of Lauds, which in Tenebrae follows the Third Nocturn of Matins, is the traditional morning prayer of the church in the western world. The word "laud" means "to sing or speak the praises of" and originally implied a formal act of worship. Customarily, Lauds included six or seven selections from the Psalter. Psalms 148-150, counted as one psalm, were always recited. In these latter psalms the word *laudate* (Latin meaning "praise") appears repeatedly. From this repetition the office derived its name. In addition to the psalms, Lauds contained an Old Testament canticle, a short responsory, the Benedictus (Canticle 4 or 16 in the Prayer Book), an anthem, the Lord's Prayer, Psalm 51, and a collect.

When they were united to form Tenebrae, the previously separate offices of Matins and Lauds were not abbreviated conspicuously. Indeed, the union of the two liturgies produced a ritual greater than the sum of its parts. Through their correlation with the systematic extinguishing of candles unique to Tenebrae, those who originated the ceremony gave a new and greater interpretive task to the psalms and canticles. As we have noted, in their new liturgical context these poignant scriptural laments serve as commentary upon the darkness that gradually enshrouds the church and ominously envelops Jesus' life during Holy Week.[7]

CONCERNING TEXTS AND MUSICAL SETTINGS

This booklet relies heavily upon several previous publications of The Church Hymnal Corporation. As noted earlier, the service of Tenebrae presented in these pages conforms to the outline found in *The Book of Occasional Services, 1991*. This version of Tenebrae is intended for use on the Wednesday evening of Holy Week only. By gathering into a single

---

[6]A responsory consists of a series of versicles and responses. The text is generally drawn from Holy Scripture.

[7]With two obvious exceptions, the traditional elements of each office are still found in the order of service presented below: Within Lauds the recitation of Psalms 148-150 has been dropped; only Psalm 150 is sung or said. Similarly, the Lord's Prayer has been omitted.

evening the themes originally assigned to the last three nights of Holy Week, the rite serves as prelude to the Prayer Book liturgies for Maundy Thursday, Good Friday and the Great Vigil of Easter.

The Tenebrae outlined in *The Book of Occasional Services* includes texts for the three readings (nine lessons) of Matins. For the sake of convenience those lections have been included in this booklet. For reasons of copyright, the Scripture readings for this booklet have been taken from the Revised Standard Version. However, other translations authorized for public worship, such as the New Revised Standard Version, may be used instead. The masculine-oriented language of St. Augustine's *Treatise* has been modified where necessary through the introduction of plural forms, simple rephrasing, and the substitution of contextually appropriate nouns (e.g., "the psalmist" or "the speaker") for gender-specific pronouns.[8]

The version of the psalms included in this booklet is the one familiar to users of The Book of Common Prayer, 1979.[9] The psalm tones are drawn from James Litton's *The Plainsong Psalter*, published by The Church Hymnal Corporation in 1988.[10] It is hoped that interested congregations will learn to sing the office. The settings are not difficult; some may be familiar. Learning to sing these ancient tones can be an enjoyable group experience. People invited to join such an activity often respond with enthusiasm.[11] Those who prefer to recite Tenebrae without singing the psalms, however, will not be hindered by the pointing or lines of music.

The plainsong setting of the Song of Hezekiah (p. 35) is adapted from a setting of Canticle 8 (C-89) found in *The Book of Canticles: Church Hymnal Series II*, 1979.

---

[8] See J. Robert Wright's guidelines for the inclusive translation or re-translation of such Latin and Greek texts in, "The Genesis of a Book," *Readings for the Daily Office from the Early Church*, 2nd printing (New York: The Church Hymnal Corporation, 1991), especially 519-523.

[9] In those instances where *The Book of Occasional Services* suggests that a psalm may be shortened (Psalms 69 and 22 in Matins, and Psalms 63 and 90 in Lauds), the full form has been given, with a clear indication of where to end the abridged version. In the case of Psalm 69, the verse numbering for the sung version differs from the numbering in the Prayer Book.

[10] Musical settings have been adapted for all of the antiphons for Tenebrae.

[11] See, "Performance Notes," in *The Plainsong Psalter*, xi, for assistance in learning to chant the office. Note in particular the remarks concerning accompaniment (xiv). Although plainsong has traditionally been sung without accompaniment, a simple keyboard accompaniment may be very useful to congregations as they incorporate Tenebrae into Holy Week.

CONCERNING THE SERVICE[12]

Although there must be enough illumination for the recitation of the office, the church should be dimly lit.[13] No special preparation of the altar itself is necessary. It may be vested in the color customarily used during Holy Week—generally passion-red or purple. In addition to the usual altar lights, however, for Tenebrae a total of fifteen candles is placed on a "hearse" (derived from the Medieval Latin word *hercia* and sometimes spelled "herse"). The hearse is a triangular frame or fifteen-branched candelabrum set upon a stand. It is to be situated in the chancel on the right (i.e., liturgical south) side of the church.

Note: There are a variety of architectural arrangements and styles in the worship spaces of our churches, and no single set of directional rubrics will suffice for every congregation. While many churches have a "traditional" layout in which the altar is in the front of the church, distinctly separate from the congregational seating area in the nave, others have been designed and built "in the round" or with the altar area surrounded on at least three sides by chairs or pews. For ease of description here, the term "chancel" is used to describe the area immediately surrounding the altar. The directions "left" and "right" are given relative to the altar as it is faced head-on from the nave in the "traditional" floor plan.

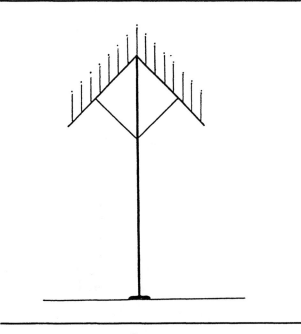

Figure 1

While several church supply companies will "special order" fifteen-branched candelabra,[14] a simple hearse may be constructed of wood. It could resemble the one pictured in Figure 1. A parishioner with skill in woodworking might be pleased to accept the challenge of building a hearse. Alternatively, your parish may already possess the liturgical hardware necessary to fashion a hearse. Two adjustable, seven-branched candelabra, for example, may be used with a pavement light (Figure 2) or with an altar candle (Figure 3) to create the

---

[12]The liturgical actions described in the following paragraphs are also outlined in the rubrics of the service. These introductory remarks are intended to provide an overview of the action and to note its symbolic content.

[13]You may wish to consider making hand-held candles available.

[14]Allow eight to ten weeks.

appearance of a hearse. If your church does not own such items, the seven-branched candelabra could be constructed of wood.

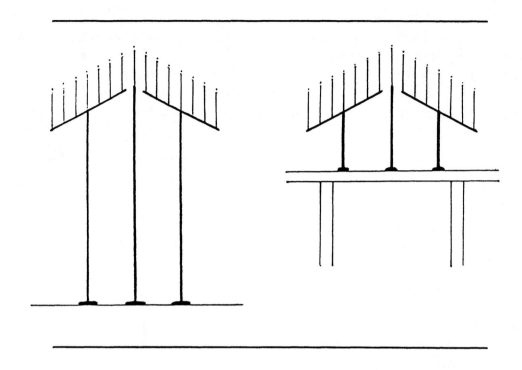

Figure 2   *Figure 3*

The officiant, acolytes and readers may vest as they ordinarily do for choir offices. There should be no musical prelude or postlude. The procession is silent; acolytes do not carry a cross or torches. The officiant may wish to offer a few explanatory remarks before the liturgy begins. There is no homily at Tenebrae. Three readers are recommended: one for the three lessons of each Nocturn. Readers should be selected carefully and be well rehearsed.

Two acolytes are needed. They may be seated on opposite sides of the chancel near the hearse. If convenient, the acolytes should alternate extinguishing the candles. The candles on the hearse are put out one-by-one after each of the first thirteen psalms and also at the end of the Song of Hezekiah.[15] The lower fourteen candles on the hearse represent the followers of Jesus. The candle at the hearse's apex symbolizes the Christ himself. As the lower hearse candles are gradually extinguished, worshipers are reminded of the disciples' disaffection and of our Lord's growing isolation during his final days. Symbolic of Jesus' steadfast love and endurance, the Christ candle remains burning throughout the service; it will be concealed for a brief time, but it is not extinguished.

---

[15]Rubrics within the service make clear when candles are to be extinguished. In general, the candles on the hearse should be extinguished from bottom to top, alternating from side to side.

During the canticle *Benedictus Dominus Deus Israel* the acolytes extinguish the altar candles and as many more lights throughout the rest of the church as is feasible.[16] Then, during the repetition of Antiphon Fifteen (which follows the Benedictus), one acolyte is to remove the burning Christ candle from the hearse and hide it behind the altar or in some other nearby location. At the same time, the other acolyte prepares to make the "loud noise" which will follow the final collect. The Christ candle remains concealed during the recitation of Psalm 51 and the concluding collect. Following the collect there is a period of silence that is interrupted by the "loud noise." The noise signifies the earthquake which occurred at the time of the resurrection. According to Matthew 28, an angel created a thunderous disturbance by rolling back the stone that covered Jesus' tomb. This dramatic occurrence prefaced the angel's announcement of Jesus' departure from the dead in the resurrection. Whatever the source—a cymbal crash, a drum roll, a book thrown to the floor—the noise should be created from a concealed position. It is to be experienced "suddenly" as it was by Mary Magdalene and the other Mary (Matthew 28:2). When this *strepitus* or signal of departure has been given, the Christ candle is brought out of hiding and returned to the top of the hearse. The ministers and people then depart in silence.

Symbolically, hiding the Christ candle recalls the apparent mastery of the powers of sin and death as Jesus gives up his life and descends into Hell; returning the candle to its place on the candelabrum foreshadows our Lord's victorious manifestation as the one enduring Light of the world.

Whether sung or said, the psalms of Tenebrae should be recited antiphonally.[17] The Book of Common Prayer defines antiphonal recitation as "the verse-by-verse alternation between groups of singers or readers—e.g., between choir and congregation, or between one side of the congregation and the other" (page 582). At Tenebrae the psalms and canticles begin and end with refrains called "antiphons." Along with the canticles, the antiphons are said or sung in unison.

The antiphonal recitation of each psalm proceeds in this way: The cantor sings the antiphon for each psalm. The congregation then joins the cantor in singing the antiphon a second time. The cantor then sings verse one alone. Those seated on the cantor's side of the church[18] then join the cantor in singing verse two. Those seated on the opposite side of the church respond by singing verse three. This alternation from side to side then continues

---

[16]Following the Benedictus the congregation will participate in reciting or singing Psalm 51. The rubrics direct that hand-held candles, if they have been distributed, need not be extinguished until this final psalm has been completed. But even then complete darkness is not recommended; after the final collect the congregation will need some light to depart the church.

[17]The canticles are said or sung in unison.

[18]For Tenebrae the congregation should, if possible, be seated so that the sides face each other.

through the last verse. After the last verse the entire congregation immediately sings the appointed antiphon again.

The Book of Occasional Services suggests several ways to shorten Tenebrae. The simplest is to omit the first two responsories of each Nocturn. When this option is exercised, the readings are not divided into lessons. In the First Nocturn, for example, the three lessons drawn from Lamentations are read consecutively and without interruption.

If a much more abbreviated version of Tenebrae is desired, it is possible to omit Nocturns Two and Three of Matins and either Psalm 90 or Psalm 143 from Lauds. When these omissions are made, two candles are extinguished after each psalm.

It is also possible to omit Nocturns Two and Three and any two of the psalms of Lauds. When this is done, only a seven-branched candelabrum is needed.

WHY INCLUDE TENEBRAE IN HOLY WEEK?

St. Paul reminds us that we are "heirs of God and joint heirs with Christ—if, in fact, we suffer with him so that we may also be glorified with him" (Romans 8:17). During Holy Week the suffering our Lord endured as he moved toward the cross is happening again liturgically. We need opportunities to share in our Lord's affliction. After the exhilaration of the Palm Sunday procession, we need to experience Jesus' week-long descent through humiliation and pain into the lonely shadows of death. Waiting for a thing to happen—whether it be good or bad—is often agonizing. Anticipation is suffering indeed. Nevertheless, we must do precisely that. We must wait. We cannot skip heedlessly from Palm Sunday to Maundy Thursday or Good Friday and still grasp the full significance of Easter. Spiritually, we need Holy Week to be intentionally "holy." We need it to be set apart. We need the week to be exhausting. Only so may we truly know the Easter truth we sing: "The strife is o'er, the battle done, the victory of life is won."

Fred C. Elwood
Rector, St. John's Episcopal Church
Olympia, Washington
February 1, 1996

ACKNOWLEDGMENTS

Many parishioners over the years have offered support and encouragement for the development of this Order of Service. The people of Ascension Church, Twin Falls, Idaho; The Church of St. Andrew, Staten Island, New York; and St. John's Church, Olympia, Washington, have all practiced and prayed Tenebrae with me. Their participation in this spiritual exercise has been a marvelous gift. I am grateful to them all. I also want to thank Dr. David Hurd, Organist and Professor of Music at The General Theological Seminary, for his helpful suggestions concerning the musical portions of the service. And, very particularly, I want to thank Dr. J. Robert Wright, St. Mark's Professor of Ecclesiastical History at The General Theological Seminary, for his most generous attention to every detail and his unfailing encouragement throughout. How fortunate I am to have such good and wise friends.

Fred C. Elwood

A NOTE FROM THE MUSICAL EDITOR

When the opportunity to participate in this arose, I eagerly accepted it as a project for an exciting seminar I was then teaching at Episcopal Divinity School ("Times and Seasons: The Church Year and *The Book of Occasional Services*"). That group of intelligent, musical students provided an ideal living laboratory for the work contained in this volume, and I am deeply grateful for all that we learned together.

I am also grateful for the privilege of making Tenebrae more accessible. Those of us who know this liturgy need no convincing that it gives far more than it requires. At the same time, those of us who have worked to introduce it are aware that fear of its complexities frequently prevents its use. Fred Elwood has done a splendid job of de-mystifying those complexities.

My goal as musical editor has been to complement him. Toward that end, the psalmody is taken directly from *The Plainsong Psalter;* as my students at EDS continue to remind me, true and full participation depends upon regularly encountering a common literature. Parishes and communities which already know and cherish *The Plainsong Psalter* begin with the advantage of this shared repertoire.

The setting of the antiphons was not so easily resolved. Despite the resurgent popularity of chant, we do not live in an age which can produce authentic plainsong. Our seminar experience validated the time-honored practice of choosing a tone for the antiphon which complements but is not identical to the tone of the primary text. Hence, the antiphons have been set as directly and simply as individual verses.

John L. Hooker

The Office of Tenebrae

The ministers enter the church in silence and proceed to their places. The Office then begins immediately with the Antiphon on the first Psalm. It is customary to sit for the Psalmody.

MATINS

THE FIRST NOCTURN

ANTIPHON ONE *Tone VII.2*

Zeal for your house has eat-en me up; the scorn of those who scorn you has fal-len up-on me.

Psalm 69 *or* Psalm 69:1-23 *Salvum me fac* *Tone III.4*

1   *Save më*, O God,
     for the waters have risen úp to mÿ neck.*
         I am sinking in deep mire,
         and there is no firm ground / for mý feet.

2   I have come ínto deep wäters, *
         and the torrent wash/es óver me.

3   I have grown weary with my crying;
     my thróat is ínflamed; *
         my eyes have failed from look/ing fór my God.

1

4   Those who hate me without a cause are more than the hairs of my head;
       my lying foes who would destróy me are míghty. *
         Must I then give back what / I néver stole?

5   O God, you knów my fóolishness, *
       and my faults are not hid/den fróm you.

6   Let not those who hope in you be put to shame through
           mé, Lord GÓD öf hosts; *
       let not those who seek you be disgraced because of
           me, O God / of Ísrael.

7   Surely, for your sake have I súffered rëproach, *
       and shame has co/vered mý face.

8   I have become a stranger tó my own kïndred, *
       an alien to my mo/ther's children.

9   Zeal for your house has éaten më up; *
       the scorn of those who scorn you has fallen / upón me.

10   I humbled mysélf with fästing, *
       but that was turned / to mý reproach.

11   I put on sáck-cloth älso,
       and became a byword / amóng them.

12   Those who sit at the gate múrmur agäïnst me, *
       and the drunkards make songs a/bóut me.

13   But as for me, thís is my práyer tö you, *
       at the time you / have sét, O LORD:

14   "In your great mércy, Ö God, *
       answer me with your / unfáiling help.

15 Save me from the mire; dó not let më sink; *
    let me be rescued from those who hate me
    and out of the / deep wáters.

16 Let not the torrent of waters wash over me,
    neither let the deep swállow më up; *
    do not let the Pit shut its mouth / upón me.

17 Answer me, O LÓRD, for your lóve ïs kind; *
    in your great compas/sion, túrn to me."

18 "Hide not your fáce from your sërvant; *
    be swift and answer me, for I / am ín distress.

19 Draw near to mé and redéëm me; *
    because of my enemies / delíver me.

20 You know my reproach, my sháme, and my díshönor; *
    my adversaries are all / in yóur sight."

21 Reproach has broken my heart, and it cánnot bë healed; *
    I looked for sympathy, but there was none,
    for comforters, but I could / find nó one.

22 They gáve me gáll tö eat, *
    and when I was thirsty, they gave me vine/gar tó drink.

(The shorter version may end here. Verse numbers are for the sung version and do not conform to the Prayer Book numbering.)

23 Let the table befóre them bé ä trap *
    and their sa/cred féasts a snare.

24 Let their eyes be darkened, that théy may nöt see, *
    and give them continual trem/bling ín their loins.

25 Pour out your indignátion upön them, *
    and let the fierceness of your anger o/vertáke them.

3

26   Let their cámp be desölate, *
       and let there be none to dwell / in théir tents.

27   For they persecute hím whom you háve stricken *
       and add to the pain of those / whom yóu have pierced.

28   Lay to their charge gúilt upön guilt, *
       and let them not receive your vin/dicátion.

29   Let them be wiped out of the bóok of the líving *
       and not be written among / the ríghteous.

30   As for me, I am afflícted and ïn pain; *
       your help, O God, will lift / me úp on high.

31   I will praise the Náme of Gód ïn song; *
       I will proclaim his greatness with / thanksgíving.

32   This will please the LORD more than an óffering of öxen, *
       more than bullocks / with hórns and hoofs.

33   The afflicted shall sée and bë glad; *
       you who seek God, / your héart shall live.

34   For the LORD listens tó the nëedy, *
       and his prisoners he / does nót despise.

35   Let the heavens and the éarth präise him, *
       the seas and all / that móves in them;

36   For God will save Zion and rebuild the cíties of Júdah; *
       they shall live there and have it in / posséssion.

37   The children of his servants wíll inhéfit it, *
       and those who love his Name / will dwéll therein.

Zeal for your house has eat-en me up; the scorn of those who scorn you has

fal-len up-on me.

The first candle (lowest on the right side) is extinguished.

A brief silence is kept.

ANTIPHON TWO   *Tone III.8*

Let them draw back and be dis - graced who take plea-sure in my mis-for-tune.

Psalm 70   *Deus, in adjutorium*   *Tone VIII.1*

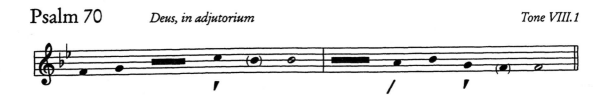

1   *Be pleased*, O God, to delíver me; *
      O LORD, make / haste to hélp me.

2   Let those who seek my life be ashamed
      and altogether dismáyed; *
          let those who take pleasure in my misfortune
          draw / back and bé disgraced.

3   Let those who say to me "Aha!" and gloat over me túrn back, *
          be/cause they áre ashamed.

4   Let all who seek you rejoice and be glád in you; *
          let those who love your salvation say for ever,
          / "Great is thé LORD!"

5 But as for me, I am poor and néedy; *
  come to me speed/ily, Ó God.

6 You are my helper and my delíverer; *
  O Lᴏʀᴅ, / do not tárry.

Aɴᴛɪᴘʜᴏɴ Tᴡᴏ *(repeated)*   *Tone III.8*

Let them draw back and be dis-graced who take plea-sure in my mis-for-tune.

The second candle (lowest on the left side) is extinguished.

A brief silence is kept.

Aɴᴛɪᴘʜᴏɴ Tʜʀᴇᴇ   *Tone IV*

A - rise, O God, main - tain my cause.

Psalm 74   *Ut quid, Deus?*   *Tone IV.4*

1 *O Göd, why have you ut/terly cást us off? *
  why is your wrath so hot against the / sheep of your pásture?*

2 Remember your congregation that you / purchased lóng ago, *
  the tribe you redeemed to be your inheritance,
  and / Mount Zion whére you dwell.

3 Turn your steps toward the / endless rúins; *
   the enemy has laid waste everything in / your sanctuáry.

4 Your adversaries roared / in your hóly place; *
   they set up their banners as / tokens of víctory.

5 They were like men coming up with axes / to a gróve of trees; *
   they broke down all your carved work with / hatchets and hámmers.

6 They set fire / to your hóly place; *
   they defiled the dwelling-place of your Name
   / and razed it tó the ground.

7 They said to themselves, "Let us destroy them / altogéther." *
   They burned down all the meeting-pla/ces of God iń the land.

8 There are no signs for us to see;
  there / is no próphet left; *
   there is not one among / us who knows hów long.

9 How long, O God, will the / adversáry scoff? *
   will the enemy blaspheme / your Name for éver?

10 Why do / you draw báck your hand? *
   why is your right hand hid/den in your bósom?

11 Yet God is my / King from áncient times, *
   victorious / in the midst óf the earth.

12 You divided the sea / by your míght *
   and shattered the heads of the dragons / upon the wáters;

13 You crushed the heads / of Levíathan *
   and gave him to the people of / the desert fór food.

14 You split open / spring and tórrent; *
    you dried up ev/er-flowing rívers.

15 Yours is the day, yours al/so the níght; *
    you established / the moon and thé sun.

16 You fixed all the / boundaries óf the earth; *
    you made both / summer and wínter.

17 Remember, O LORD, how the en/emy scóffed, *
    how a foolish / people despísed your Name.

18 Do not hand over the life of your / dove to wíld beasts; *
    never forget / the lives of yóur poor.

19 Look up/on your cóvenant; *
    the dark places of the earth / are haunts of víolence.

20 Let not the oppressed / turn awáy ashamed; *
    let the poor / and needy práise your Name.

21 Arise, O / God, maintáin your cause; *
    remember how fools / revile you áll day long.

22 Forget not the clamor of your / adversáries, *
    the unending tumult of those who / rise up agáinst you.

ANTIPHON THREE *(repeated)*   *Tone IV*

A - rise,   O God,   main - tain   my   cause.

The third candle (second level, right side) is extinguished.

A brief silence is kept.

Versicle	Deliver me, my God, from the hand of the wicked:
Response	From the clutches of the evildoer and the oppressor.

All stand for silent prayer.

The first Reader then moves to the lectern, pulpit, or other designated location for the first reading. When the Reader is in position, everyone else sits down. The reading, which is divided into three lessons, is announced before the first lesson only. There are no closing statements after the lessons. The first three lessons are drawn from the Lamentations of Jeremiah the Prophet.

LESSON ONE

A Reading from the Lamentations of Jeremiah the Prophet. [1:1–14]

Aleph. How solitary lies the city, once so full of people! How like a widow has she become, she that was great among the nations! She that was queen among the cities has now become a vassal.

Beth. She weeps bitterly in the night, tears run down her cheeks; among all her lovers she has none to comfort her; all her friends have dealt treacherously with her; they have become her enemies.

Gimel. Judah has gone into the misery of exile and of hard servitude; she dwells now among the nations, but finds no resting place; all her pursuers overtook her in the midst of her anguish.

Daleth. The roads to Zion mourn, because none come to the solemn feasts; all her gates are desolate, her priests groan and sigh; her virgins are afflicted, and she is in bitterness.

He. Her adversaries have become her masters, her enemies prosper; because the Lord has punished her for the multitude of her rebellions; her children are gone, driven away as captives by the enemy.

Jerusalem, Jerusalem, return to the Lord your God!

After the lesson the Reader sits down. The Responsories are recited seated.

A brief silence is kept before the Responsory is said.

RESPONSORY ONE   *In monte Oliveti*

Officiant	On the mount of Olives Jesus prayed to the Father:
People	Father, if it be possible, let this cup pass from me.
	The spirit indeed is willing, but the flesh is weak.
Officiant	Watch and pray, that you may not enter into temptation.
People	The spirit indeed is willing, but the flesh is weak.

The Reader returns to the appointed place for the next lesson.

LESSON TWO

Waw. And from Daughter Zion all her majesty has departed; her princes have become like stags that can find no pasture, and that run without strength before the hunter.

Zayin. Jerusalem remembers in the days of her affliction and bitterness all the precious things that were hers from the days of old; when her people fell into the hand of the foe, and there was none to help her; the adversary saw her, and mocked at her downfall.

Heth. Jerusalem has sinned greatly, therefore she has become a thing unclean; all who honored her despise her, for they have seen her nakedness; and now she sighs, and turns her face away.

Teth. Uncleanness clung to her skirts, she took no thought of her doom; therefore her fall is terrible, she has no comforter. "O Lord, behold my affliction, for the enemy has triumphed."

Jerusalem, Jerusalem, return to the Lord your God!

After the lesson the Reader sits down. The Responsories are recited seated.

A brief silence is kept before the Responsory is said.

RESPONSORY TWO   *Tristis est anima mea*

Officiant	My soul is very sorrowful, even to the point of death;
People	remain here, and watch with me.
	Now you shall see the crowd who will surround me;
	you will flee, and I will go to be offered up for you.
Officiant	Behold, the hour is at hand, and the Son of Man is
	betrayed into the hands of sinners.
People	You will flee, and I will go to be offered up for you.

The Reader returns to the appointed place for the conclusion of the lesson.

LESSON THREE

Yodh. The adversary has stretched out his hand to seize all her precious things; she has seen the Gentiles invade her sanctuary, those whom you had forbidden to enter your congregation.

Kaph. All her people groan as they search for bread; they sell their own children for food to revive their strength. "Behold, O Lord, and consider, for I am now beneath contempt!"

Lamedh. Is it nothing to you, all you who pass by? Behold and see if there is any sorrow like my sorrow, which was brought upon me, which the Lord inflicted, on the day of his burning anger.

Mem. From on high he sent fire, into my bones it descended; he spread a net for my feet, and turned me back; he has left me desolate and faint all the day long.

Nun. My transgressions were bound into a yoke; by his hand they were fastened together; their yoke is upon my neck; he has caused my strength to fail. The Lord has delivered me into their hands, against whom I am not able to stand up.

Jerusalem, Jerusalem, return to the Lord your God!

After the lesson the Reader sits down.

A brief silence is kept before the Responsory is said.

RESPONSORY THREE   *Ecce vidimus eum*

Officiant	Lo, we have seen him without beauty or majesty,
People	with no looks to attract our eyes.
	He bore our sins and grieved for us,
	he was wounded for our transgressions,
	and by his scourging we are healed.
Officiant	Surely he has borne our griefs and carried our sorrows:
People	And by his scourging we are healed.

A brief silence is kept.

The Second Nocturn

The kings of the earth rise up in re - volt, and the prin - ces plot to - ge - ther,

a - gainst the Lord and a - gainst his A - noin - ted.

Psalm 2   *Quare fremuerunt gentes?*   *Tone VIII.1*

1   *Why are* the nations in an úproar? *
       Why do the peoples / mutter émpty threats?

2   Why do the kings of the earth rise up in revolt,
    and the princes plot togéther, *
       against the LORD and against / his Anóinted?

3   "Let us break their yoke," they sáy; *
       "let us cast / off their bónds from us."

4   He whose throne is in heaven is láughing; *
       the Lord has them / in derísion.

5   Then he speaks to them in his wráth, *
       and his rage fills / them with térror.

6   "I myself have sét my king *
       upon my holy / hill of Zíon."

7   Let me announce the decree of the LÓRD: *
       he said to me, "You are my Son;
       this day have / I begótten you.

8   Ask of me, and I will give you the nations for your inhéritance *
      and the ends of the earth for / your posséssion.

9   You shall crush them with an irón rod *
      and shatter them like a / piece of póttery."

10   And now, you kíngs, be wise; *
      be warned, you / rulers óf the earth.

11   Submit to the LÓRD with fear, *
      and with trembling / bow befóre him;

12   Lest he be angry and you pérish; *
      for his wrath is / quickly kíndled.

13   Happy are they áll *
      who take / refuge ín him!

ANTIPHON FOUR *(repeated)*   *Tone VI*

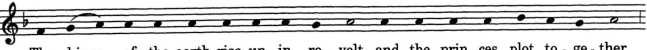

The kings of the earth rise up in re - volt, and the prin - ces plot to - ge - ther,

a - gainst the Lord and a - gainst his A - noin - ted.

The fourth candle (second level, left side) is extinguished.

ANTIPHON FIVE   *Tone III.5*

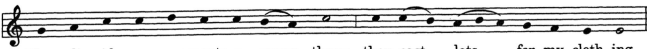

They di - vide my gar - ments a - mong them; they cast lots for my cloth - ing.

1   *My God*, my God, why have / you forsáken me? *
     and are so far from my cry
     and from the / words of mÿ d́istress?

2   O my God, I cry in the daytime, but you / do not ánswer; *
     by night as well, / but I f́ind n̈ó rest.

3   Yet you / are the Hóly One, *
     enthroned upon the / praises ö́f Ísräel.

4   Our forefathers / put their trúst in you; *
     they trusted, and / you delïv́ëred them.

5   They cried out to you and / were deĺivered; *
     they trusted in you and / were not p̈ut ẗó shame.

6   But as for me, I am a / worm and nó man, *
     scorned by all and / despised bÿ the ṕëople.

7   All who see me laugh / me to scórn; *
     they curl their lips and / wag their hëads, s̈áying,

8   "He trusted in the LORD; let / him deĺiver him; *
     let him rescue him, if / he del̈ights ́ïn him."

9   Yet you are he who took me out / of the wómb, *
     and kept me safe up/on my mötḧér's breast.

10   I have been entrusted to you ever since / I was bórn; *
     you were my God when I was still / in my mötḧér's womb.

11   Be not far from me, for trou/ble is néar, *
     and / there is n̈óne ẗö help.

12   Many young / bulls encircle me; *
        strong bulls of / Bashan surround me.

13   They open / wide their jaws at me, *
        like a ravening / and a roaring lion.

14   I am poured out like water;
        all my / bones are out of joint; *
           my heart within my / breast is melting wax.

15   My mouth is dried out like a pot-sherd;
        my tongue sticks to the roof / of my mouth; *
           and you have laid me / in the dust of the grave.

16   Packs of dogs close me in,
        and gangs of evildoers cir/cle around me; *
           they pierce my hands and my feet;
           / I can count all my bones.

17   They stare / and gloat over me; *
        they divide my garments among them;
        they cast / lots for my clothing.

18   Be not / far away, O Lord; *
        you are my strength; / hasten to help me.

19   Save me / from the sword, *
        my life / from the power of the dog.

20   Save me / from the lion's mouth, *
        my wretched body / from the horns of wild bulls.

21   I will declare your Name / to my brethren; *
        in the midst of the congrega/tion I will praise you.

22 Praise the LORD, / you that féar him; *

    stand in awe of him, O offspring of Israel;

    all you of / Jacob's líne, gíve glöry.

23 For he does not despise nor abhor the poor in their poverty;

    neither does he / hide his fáce from them; *

    but when they / cry to hïm hé hëars them.

24 My praise is of him in the / great assémbly; *

    I will perform my vows in the presence of / those who wörshïp him.

25 The poor shall eat and be satisfied,

    and those who seek the / LORD shall práise him: *

    "May / your heart lïve fór ëver!"

26 All the ends of the earth shall remember and turn / to the LÓRD, *

    and all the families of the na/tions shall böw befo̊rë him.

27 For kingship belongs / to the LÓRD; *

    he / rules över thé nätions.

28 To him alone all who sleep in the earth bow / down in wórship; *

    all who go down to the / dust fall befo̊rë him.

29 My soul shall live for him;

    my descen/dants shall sérve him; *

    they shall be known / as the LÖRD's fór ëver.

30 They shall come and make known to a / people yét unborn *

    the saving / deeds that hë hàs done.

ANTIPHON FIVE *(repeated)* Tone III.5

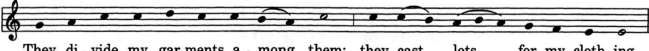

They di - vide my gar - ments a - mong them; they cast lots for my cloth - ing.

The fifth candle (right side) is extinguished.

A brief silence is kept.

ANTIPHON SIX *Tone III.8*

False wit-nes-ses have ris-en up a-gainst me, and al-so those who speak mal-ice.

Psalm 27 *Dominus illuminatio* *Tone VIII.1*

1a   *The LORD is my light and my salvátion;*
       — / whom then sháll I fear? *

b   the LORD is the strength of my lífe;
       of whom then / shall I bé afraid?

2   When evildoers came upon me to eat up my flésh, *
       it was they, my foes and my adversaries, who / stumbled ánd fell.

3   Though an army should encamp agáinst me, *
       yet my heart / shall not bé afraid;

4   And though war should rise up agáinst me, *
       yet will I / put my trúst in him.

5   One thing have I asked of the LORD;
       one thing I seek; *
       that I may dwell in the house of the LORD all the / days of mý life;

6   To behold the fair beauty of the LÓRD *
       and to seek him / in his témple.

7 For in the day of trouble he shall keep me safe in his shélter; *
      he shall hide me in the secrecy of his dwelling
      and set me / high upón a rock.

8 Even now he lifts úp my head *
      above my enemies / round abóut me.

9 Therefore I will offer in his dwelling an oblation
   with sounds of great gládness; *
      I will sing and make / music tó the LORD.

10 Hearken to my voice, O LORD, when I cáll; *
      have mercy on / me and ánswer me.

11 You speak in my heart and say, "Séek my face." *
      Your / face, LORD, wíll I seek.

12 Hide not your fáce from me, *
      nor turn away your servant / in displéasure.

13 You have been my helper;
    cast me nót away; *
      do not forsake me, O God of / my salvátion.

14 Though my father and my mother forsáke me, *
      the LORD / will sustáin me.

15 Show me your way, O LÓRD; *
      lead me on a level path, because / of my énemies.

16 Deliver me not into the hand of my adversáries, *
      for false witnesses have risen up against me,
      and also those / who speak málice.

17 What if I had not believed
    that I should see the goodness of the LÓRD *
      in the land / of the líving!

18   O tarry and await the LORD's pleasure;

        be strong, and he shall comfort yóur heart; *

            wait pa/tiently fór the LORD.

ANTIPHON SIX *(repeated)*   *Tone III.8*

False wit - nes - ses. have ris - en up a - gainst me,   and al - so those who speak mal - ice.

The sixth candle (left side) is extinguished.

A brief silence is kept.

Versicle   They divide my garments among them:
Response   They cast lots for my clothing.

All stand for silent prayer.

The second Reader then moves to the designated location for the second series of lessons. When the Reader is in position, everyone else sits down. The reading, drawn from patristic literature, is announced prior to lesson four only. There are no closing statements after the lessons.

LESSON FOUR

A Reading from the Treatise of Saint Augustine the Bishop on the Psalms.
[Vulgate Psalm 54. Prayer Book Psalm 55:1,2,10c]

"Hear my prayer, O God; do not hide yourself from my petition. Listen to me and answer me. I mourn in my trial and am troubled."

These are the words of one disquieted, in trouble and anxiety, praying under much suffering, desiring to be delivered from evil. Let us now see under what evil the psalmist lies; when the speaker begins, let us be witnesses, that, by sharing the tribulation, we may also join in the prayer.

"I mourn in my trial," the poet says, "and am troubled."

When does this mourning occur? When is this trouble encountered? The speaker says, "In my trial." The psalmist has in mind a suffering caused by those who are wicked. This suffering is described as "my trial." Do not think that the evil are in the world for no purpose, and that God makes no good use of them. The wicked live, either that they may be corrected, or that through them the righteous may be tried and tested.

After the lesson the Reader sits down.

A brief silence is kept before the Responsory is said.

RESPONSORY FOUR   *Tamquam ad latronem*

Officiant   Have you come out as against a robber,
People   with swords and clubs to capture me?
                Day after day I sat in the temple teaching,
                and you did not seize me;
                but now, behold, you scourge me,
                and lead me away to be crucified.
Officiant   When they had laid hands on Jesus and were holding
                him, he said:
People   Day after day I sat in the temple teaching,
                and you did not seize me;
                but now, behold, you scourge me,
                and lead me away to be crucified.

The Reader returns to the appointed place for the next lesson.

LESSON FIVE

Would that those who now test us were converted and tried with us; yet though they continue to try us, let us not hate them, for we do not know whether any of them will persist to the end in their evil ways. And most of the time, when you think you are hating your enemy, you are hating your friend without knowing it.

Only the devil and the angels of the evil one are shown to us in the Holy Scriptures as doomed to eternal fire. It is only their amendment that is hopeless, and against them we wage a hidden battle. For this battle the Apostle Paul arms us, saying, "We are not contending against flesh and blood," that is, not against human beings whom we see, "but against the principalities, against the powers, against the rulers of the darkness of this world." So that you may not think that demons are the rulers of heaven and earth, the Apostle says, "of the darkness of this world."

Paul says, "of the world," meaning the lovers of the world—of the "world," meaning the ungodly and wicked—the "world" of which the Gospel says, "And the world knew him not."

After the lesson the Reader sits down.

A brief silence is kept before the Responsory is said.

20

Officiant	Darkness covered the whole land
	when Jesus had been crucified;
People	and about the ninth hour he cried with a loud voice:
	My God, my God, why have you forsaken me?
	And he bowed his head and handed over his spirit.
Officiant	Jesus, crying with a loud voice, said:
	Father, into your hands I commend my spirit.
People	And he bowed his head and handed over his spirit.

LESSON SIX

"For I have seen unrighteousness and strife in the city."

See the glory of the cross itself. On the brow of kings that cross is now placed, the cross which enemies once mocked. Its power is shown in the result. Jesus has conquered the world, not by steel, but by wood. The wood of the cross seemed a fitting object of scorn to his enemies, and standing before that wood they wagged their heads, saying, "If you are the Son of God, come down from the cross." Jesus stretched out his hands to an unbelieving and rebellious people. If one is just who lives by faith, one who does not have faith is unrighteous. Therefore when the psalmist says "unrighteousness," understand that it is unbelief. The Lord then saw unrighteousness and strife in the city, and stretched out his hands to an unbelieving and rebellious people. And yet, looking upon them, he said, "Father, forgive them, for they know not what they do."

After the lesson the Reader sits down.

A brief silence is kept before the Responsory is said.

RESPONSORY SIX   *Ecce quomodo moritur*

Officiant	See how the righteous one perishes,
People	and no one takes it to heart.
	The righteous are taken away, and no one understands.
	From the face of evil the righteous one is taken away,
	and his memory shall be in peace.
Officiant	Like a sheep before its shearers is mute,
	so he opened not his mouth.
	By oppression and judgment he was taken away:
People	And his memory shall be in peace.

A brief silence is kept.

THE THIRD NOCTURN

ANTIPHON SEVEN   Tone V.3

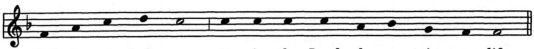

God is my help - er; it is the Lord who sus - tains my life.

Psalm 54   *Deus, in nomine*   Tone I.2

1 *Save më, O Gód, by yóur Name;* *
  in your / might, deféňd my cäuse.

2 —Héar my práyer, O God; *
  give ear to the / words of m̈ÿ möuth.

3 For the arrogant have risen up against me,
  and the rúthless have sóught my life, *
   those who have / no regářd for Göd.

4 Behold, Gód is my hélper; *
  it is the Lord / who sustáins my l̈ife.

5 Render evil to thóse who spý on me; *
  in your faithful/ness, deströÿ them.

6 I will offer you a fréewill sácrifice *
  and praise your Name, O / LORD, for ït is göod.

7 For you have rescued me from évery tróuble, *
  and my eye has seen the / ruin öf my föes.

ANTIPHON SEVEN *(repeated)*   Tone V.3

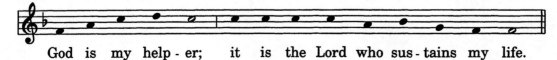

God is my help - er; it is the Lord who sus - tains my life.

22

The seventh candle (right side) is extinguished.

A brief silence is kept.

ANTIPHON EIGHT *Tone VI*

At Sa - lem is his ta - ber - nac - le, and his dwel - ling is in Zi - on.

Psalm 76   *Notus in Judaea* *Tone V.3*

1   *In Ju*dah is Gód known; *
      his Name is gréat in Ísrael.

2   At Salem is his tabernácle, *
      and his dwelling iś in Źion.

3   There he broke the flashing árrows, *
      the shield, the sword, and the weapóns of báttle.

4   How glorious yóu are! *
      more splendid than the everlásting móuntains!

5   The strong of heart have been despoiled;
   they sink ińto sleep; *
      none of the warriórs can líft a hand.

6   At your rebuke, O God of Jácob, *
      both horse and ŕider líe stunned.

7   What terror yóu inspire! *
      who can stand before you when yóu are ángry?

8   From heaven you pronounced júdgment; *
      the earth was afráid and wás still;

9   When God rose up to júdgment *
       and to save all the oppréssed of thé earth.

10   Truly, wrathful Edom will gíve you thanks, *
       and the remnant of Hamáth will kéep your feasts.

11   Make a vow to the LORD your God and kéep it; *
       let all around him bring gifts to him who is wórthy tó be feared.

12   He breaks the spirit of prínces, *
       and strikes terror in the kíngs of thé earth.

ANTIPHON EIGHT *(repeated)*   *Tone VI*

At Sa - lem is his ta - ber - nac - le, and his dwel - ling is in Zi - on.

The eighth candle (left side) is extinguished.

A brief silence is kept.

ANTIPHON NINE   *Tone VII.3*

I   have   be - come like one who has no strength, lost a - mong the dead.

Psalm 88   *Domine, Deus*   *Tone I.7*

1   *O LORD, my Gód, my Sávior, *
       by day and / night I crÿ to yöü.*

2   Let my prayer enter ínto your présence; *
       incline your ear to my / lamentätiön.

24

3   For I am full of trouble; *
        my life is at the / brink of the grave.

4   I am counted among those who go down to the Pit; *
        I have become like one / who has no strength;

5   — Lost among the dead, *
        like the slain / who lie in the grave,

6   Whom you remember no more, *
        for they are / cut off from your hand.

7   You have laid me in the depths of the Pit, *
        in dark places, / and in the abyss.

8   Your anger weighs upon me heavily, *
        and all your great waves / overwhelm me.

9   You have put my friends far from me;
        you have made me to be abhorred by them; *
        I am in prison and / cannot get free.

10   My sight has failed me because of trouble; *
        LORD, I have called upon you daily;
        I have stretched / out my hands to you.

11   Do you work wonders for the dead? *
        will those who have died stand / up and give you thanks?

12   Will your loving-kindness be declared in the grave? *
        your faithfulness in the land / of destruction?

13   Will your wonders be known in the dark? *
        or your righteousness in the country where all / is forgotten?

14   But as for me, O LORD, I cry to you for help; *

          in the morning my prayer / comes before you.

15   LORD, why have you rejected me? *

          why have you hid/den your face from me?

16   Ever since my youth, I have been wretched and at the point of death; *

          I have borne your terrors / with a troubled mind.

17   Your blazing anger has swept over me; *

          your terrors / have destroyed me;

18   They surround me all day long like a flood; *

          they encompass / me on every side.

19   My friend and my neighbor you have put away from me, *

          and darkness is my on/ly companion.

ANTIPHON NINE *(repeated)*   *Tone VII.3*

I have become like one who has no strength, lost among the dead.

The ninth candle (right side) is extinguished.

A brief silence is kept.

Versicle   He has made me dwell in darkness:

Response   Like the dead of long ago.

All stand for a brief silent prayer.

The third Reader then moves to the designated location for the third series of lessons. When the Reader is in place, everyone else sits down. The reading, drawn from the New Testament, is announced prior to lesson seven only. There are no closing statements after the lessons.

LESSON SEVEN

A Reading from the Letter to the Hebrews. [4:15—5:10; 9:11-15]

We do not have a high priest who is unable to sympathize with our weaknesses, but one who in every respect has been tempted as we are, yet without sinning. Let us then with confidence draw near to the throne of grace, that we may receive mercy and find grace to help in time of need. For every high priest chosen from among men is appointed to act on behalf of men in relation to God, to offer gifts and sacrifices for sins. He can deal gently with the ignorant and wayward, since he himself is beset with weakness. Because of this he is bound to offer sacrifice for his own sins as well as for those of the people.

After the lesson the Reader sits down.

A brief silence is kept before the Responsory is said.

RESPONSORY SEVEN   *Eram quasi agnus*

Officiant	I was like a trusting lamb led to the slaughter.
People	I did not know it was against me that they devised schemes, saying, Let us destroy the tree with its fruit; let us cut him off from the land of the living.
Officiant	All my enemies whispered together against me, and devised evil against me, saying:
People	Let us destroy the tree with its fruit; let us cut him off from the land of the living.

The Reader returns to the appointed place for the next lesson.

LESSON EIGHT

And one does not take the honor upon himself, but he is called by God, just as Aaron was. So also, Christ did not exalt himself to be made a high priest, but was appointed by him who said to him, "You are my Son, this day have I begotten you;" as he says also in another place, "You are a priest for ever after the order of Melchizedek." In the days of his flesh, Jesus offered up prayers and supplications, with loud cries and tears, to him who was able to save him from death, and he was heard for his godly fear. Although he was a Son, he learned obedience through what he suffered; and, being made perfect, he became the source of eternal salvation to all who obey him, being designated by God a high priest after the order of Melchizedek.

After the lesson the Reader sits down.

A brief silence is kept before the Responsory is said.

RESPONSORY EIGHT   *Velum templi*

Officiant	The veil of the temple was torn in two,
People	and the earth shook,
	and the thief from the cross cried out,
	Lord, remember me when you come into your kingdom.
Officiant	The rocks were split, the tombs were opened,
	and many bodies of the saints who slept were raised:
People	And the earth shook,
	and the thief from the cross cried out,
	Lord, remember me when you come into your kingdom.

The Reader returns to the appointed place for the conclusion of the reading.

LESSON NINE

But when Christ appeared as a high priest of the good things that are to come, then, through the greater and more perfect tent (not made with hands, that is, not of this creation), he entered once for all into the Holy Place, taking not the blood of goats and calves but his own blood, thus securing an eternal redemption. For if the sprinkling of defiled persons with the blood of goats and bulls and with the ashes of a heifer sanctifies for the purification of the flesh, how much more shall the blood of Christ, who through the eternal Spirit offered himself without blemish to God, purify your conscience from dead works to serve the living God. Therefore he is the mediator of a new covenant, so that those who are called may receive the promised eternal inheritance.

After the lesson the Reader sits down.

A brief silence is kept before the Responsory is said.

RESPONSORY NINE   *Sepulto Domino*

Officiant	When the Lord was buried, they sealed the tomb,
People	rolling a great stone to the door of the tomb;
	and they stationed soldiers to guard him.
Officiant	The chief priests gathered before Pilate,
	and petitioned him:
People	And they stationed soldiers to guard him.

A brief silence is kept.

LAUDS

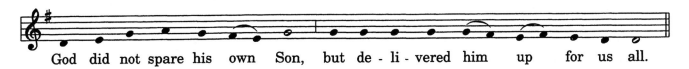

God did not spare his own Son, but de - li - vered him up for us all.

Psalm 63 *or* Psalm 63:1-8   *Deus, Deus meus*   *Tone II.1*

1   *O God*, you are my God; eagerly I seek you; *
        my soul thirsts for you, my flesh faints for you,
        as in a barren and dry land where there is / no water.

2   Therefore I have gazed upon you in your holy place, *
        that I might behold your power and / your glory.

3   For your loving-kindness is better than life itself; *
        my lips / shall give you praise.

4   So will I bless you as long as I live *
        and lift up my hands / in your Name.

5   My soul is content, as with marrow and fatness, *
        and my mouth praises you / with joyful lips,

6   When I remember you upon my bed, *
        and meditate on you in the / night watches.

7   For you have been my helper, *
        and under the shadow of your wings / I will rejoice.

8   My soul clings to you; *
        your right / hand holds me fast.

(The shorter version may end here.)

9   May those who seek my life to destróy it *
        go down into the depths / of thé earth;

10   Let them fall upon the edge of the swórd, *
        and let them be food / for jáckals.

11   But the king will rejoice in God;
        all those who swear by him wíll be glad; *
          for the mouth of those who speak / lies sháll be stopped.

ANTIPHON TEN *(repeated)*   *Tone III.4*

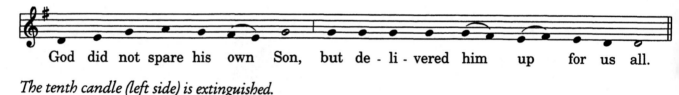

God did not spare his own Son, but de - li - vered him up for us all.

The tenth candle (left side) is extinguished.

A brief silence is kept.

ANTIPHON ELEVEN   *Tone II.2*

He was led like a lamb to the slaugh-ter, and he o - pened not his mouth.

Psalm 90 *or* Psalm 90:1–12   *Domine, refugium*   *Tone VIII.1*

1   *Lord, you* have been our réfuge *
        from one generation / to anóther.

2   Before the mountains were brought forth,
        or the land and the éarth were born, *
          from age / to age yóu are God.

3   You turn us back to the dúst and say, *
       "Go / back, O chíld of earth."

4   For a thousand years in your sight are like yesterday when ít is past *
       and like a / watch in thé night.

5   You sweep us away like a dréam; *
       we fade away sud/denly líke the grass.

6   In the morning it is green and flóurishes; *
       in the evening it is dried / up and wíthered.

7   For we consume away in your displéasure; *
       we are afraid because of your wrathful / indignátion.

8   Our iniquities you have set befóre you, *
       and our secret sins in the light / of your cóuntenance.

9   When you are angry, all our dáys are gone: *
       we bring our years to an / end like á sigh.

10   The span of our life is seventy years,
       perhaps in strength even éighty; *
         yet the sum of them is but labor and sorrow,
         for they pass away quick/ly and wé are gone.

11   Who regards the power of your wráth? *
       who rightly fears your / indignátion?

12   So teach us to number our dáys *
       that we may apply our / hearts to wísdom.

(The shorter version may end here.)

13 Return, O Lord; how long will you tárry? *
    be gracious / to your sérvants.

14 Satisfy us by your loving-kindness in the mórning; *
    so shall we rejoice and be glad all the / days of óur life.

15 Make us glad by the measure of the days that you afflícted us *
    and the years in which we suf/fered advérsity.

16 Show your servants your wórks *
    and your splendor / to their chíldren.

17 May the graciousness of the Lord our God be upón us; *
    prosper the work of our hands;
    pros/per our hándiwork.

ANTIPHON ELEVEN *(repeated)*   *Tone II.2*

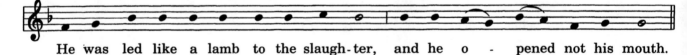

He was led like a lamb to the slaugh-ter, and he o - pened not his mouth.

The eleventh candle (right side) is extinguished.

A brief silence is kept.

ANTIPHON TWELVE   *Tone VI*

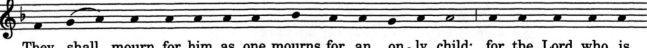

They shall mourn for him as one mourns for an on-ly child; for the Lord, who is

with - out sin is slain.

1   Lord, hëar my prayer,
    and in your faithfulness heed my sup/plicátions; *
        answer me / in yöur ríghteousness.

2   Enter not into judgment with / your sérvant, *
        for in your sight shall no one liv/ing bë jústified.

3   For my enemy has sought my life;
    he has crushed / me tó the ground; *
        he has made me live in dark places like those / who äre lóng dead.

4   My spirit faints / withiń me; *
        my heart within / me ïs désolate.

5   I remember the time past;
    I muse up/on áll your deeds; *
        I consider the / works öf yóur hands.

6   I spread out / my hánds to you; *
        my soul gasps to you / like ä thírsty land.

7   O Lord, make haste to answer me; my spir/it fáils me; *
        do not hide your face from me
        or I shall be like those who / go döwn tó the Pit.

8   Let me hear of your loving-kindness in the morning,
    for I put / my trúst in you; *
        show me the road that I must walk,
        for I lift / up mÿ sóul to you.

9   Deliver me from my ene/mies, Ó Lord, *
        for I flee to / you för réfuge.

10   Teach me to do what pleases you, for / you áre my God; *
        let your good Spirit lead / me ön lével ground.

11   Revive me, O Lord, for / your Náme's sake; *
        for your righteousness' sake, bring me / out öf tróuble.

12   Of your goodness, destroy my enemies
        and bring all / my fóes to naught, *
        for truly I / am yöur sérvant.

ANTIPHON TWELVE *(repeated)*   *Tone VI*

They shall mourn for him as one mourns for an on-ly child; for the Lord, who is

with - out sin is slain.

The twelfth candle (left side) is extinguished.

A brief silence is kept.

ANTIPHON THIRTEEN   *Tonus Peregrinus*

From the gates of hell, O Lord, de-li-ver my soul.

Cantor

1. In my despair I said, "In the noonday of my life I must de - part; *

Unison

my unspent years are summoned to the por - tals of death."

2. And I said, "No more shall I see the Lord in the land of the liv - ing, *

never more look on my kind among dwel-lers on earth. 3. My house is pulled down and

I am un - cov - ered, * as when a shep-herd strikes his tent. 4. My life is rolled up

like a bolt of cloth, * the threads cut off from the loom. 5. Between sunrise and sunset

my life is brought to an end; * I cower and hope for the dawn. 6. Like a lion he has

crushed all my bones; * like a swallow or thrush I utter plaintive cries;

I mourn like a dove. 7. My weary eyes look up to you; * Lord, be my refuge in

my af - flic - tion." 8. But what can I say? for he has spo-ken;* it is he who has done this.

9. Slow and halting are my steps all my days,* because of the bitterness of my spi - rit.

10. O Lord, I recounted all these things to you and you res- cued me; * when entreated, you re-stored my

life. 11. I know now that my bitterness was for my good, * for you held me back from the pit of de -

struc- tion, you cast all my sins be - hind you. 12. The grave does not thank you nor death give

you praise; * nor do those at the brink of the grave hang on your pro - mis-es. 13. It is the living,

O Lord, the living who give you thanks as I do this day;* and parents speak of your faithfulness

to their chil - dren. 14. You, Lord, are my Sa - vior; * I will praise you with stringed

instruments all the days of my life, in the house of the Lord.

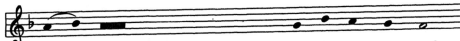

From   the gates of hell, O Lord, de - li - ver my soul.

The thirteenth candle (right side) is extinguished.

A brief silence is kept.

ANTIPHON FOURTEEN   *Tone I.4*

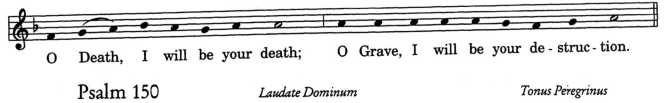

O Death, I will be your death;   O Grave, I will be your de - struc - tion.

Psalm 150   *Laudate Dominum*   *Tonus Peregrinus*

1   *Praise* God in / his holy témple; *
        praise him in the firmament / of his powër.

2   Praise / him for his míghty acts; *
        praise him for his ex/cellént greatnëss.

3   Praise him with the / blast of the rám's-horn; *
        praise him with / lyre ánd härp.

4   Praise him / with timbrel ánd dance; *
        praise him with / strings ánd pïpe.

5   Praise him with / resounding cýmbals; *
        praise him with loud-/ clangíng cymbäls.

6   Let ev/erything that hás breath *
        — / praise thé LÖRD.

ANTIPHON FOURTEEN *(repeated)*   *Tone I.4*

O Death, I will be your death;   O Grave, I will be your de - struc - tion.

The fourteenth candle (left side) is extinguished.

A brief silence is kept.

Versicle   My flesh also shall rest in hope:
Response   You will not let your holy One see corruption.

All stand. During the singing of the following Canticle, the candles at the Altar, and as many throughout the church as possible (except the one remaining at the top of the triangular candelabrum), are extinguished. If people are holding individual candles, they may keep them burning until Psalm 51 has been sung or said.

ANTIPHON FIFTEEN   Tone II.2

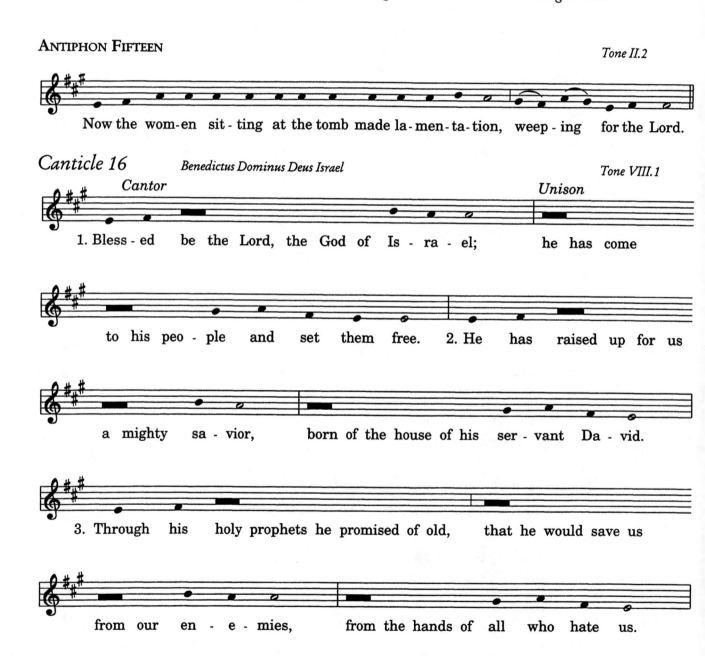

Canticle 16   *Benedictus Dominus Deus Israel*   Tone VIII.1

4. He prom - ised to show mercy to our fa - thers and to remember his

ho - ly cov - e - nant. 5. This was the oath he swore to our father

A - bra - ham, to set us free from the hands of our en - e - mies,

6. Free to worship him with - out fear, holy and righteous in his sight all the

days of our life. 7. You, my child, shall be called the prophet of the Most High,

for you will go before the Lord to pre - pare his way, 8. To give

his people knowledge of sal - va - tion by the for - give - ness of their sins.

9. In the tender compassion of our God the dawn from on high shall

break up - on us, 10. To shine on those who dwell in darkness and the

shadow of death, and to guide our feet in - to the way of peace.

During the repetition of Antiphon Fifteen (below) the Christ candle at the top of the candelabrum is hidden behind the Altar or in some other nearby place. It is not extinguished. Preparations are also made for the noise that will follow the final Collect.

ANTIPHON FIFTEEN *(repeated)*   Tone II.2

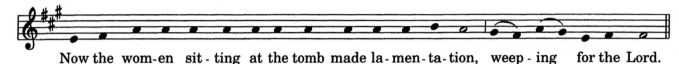

Now the wom-en sit-ting at the tomb made la-men-ta-tion, weep-ing for the Lord.

All kneel for the singing or recitation of the following anthem.

Christus factus est   Tone I.7

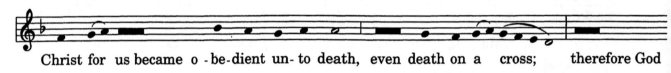

Christ for us became o-be-dient un-to death, even death on a cross; therefore God

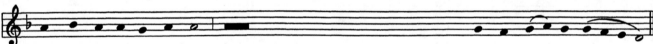

has high-ly ex-al-ted him and bestowed on him the Name which is a-bove ev-ery Name.

A brief silence is kept.

The following Psalm is then sung or said quietly. If it is sung, it is customary to monotone alternate verses.

Psalm 51   *Miserere mei, Deus*   Tone IV.1

1   *Have mërcy on me, O God, according to your / loving-kíndness; ***
    in your great compassion / blot out mÿ offênses.

2   Wash me through and through / from my wíckedness *
    and / cleanse me fröm mÿ sin.

3   For I know / my transgréssions, *
        and my sin is / ever befŏre me.

4   Against you only / have I sinned *
        and done what is / evil in yŏur sight.

5   And so you are justified / when you spéak *
        and up/right in yöur judgment.

6   Indeed, I have been wicked / from my birth, *
        a sinner / from my mŏther's womb.

7   For behold, you look for truth / deep within me, *
        and will make me understand / wisdom sĕcretly.

8   Purge me from my sin, / and I shall be pure; *
        wash me, and I / shall be clean indeed.

9   Make me hear of / joy and gládness, *
        that the body you have / broken mäy rĕjoice.

10   Hide your face / from my sins *
        and blot out / all my iniquities.

11   Create in me / a clean héart, O God, *
        and renew a right / spirit within me.

12   Cast me not away / from your présence *
        and take not your / holy Spirit from me.

13   Give me the joy of your / saving hélp again *
        and sustain me with your / bountiful Spirit.

14   I shall teach your ways / to the wicked, *
        and sinners / shall return tö you.

15   Deliver / me from déath, O God, *
        and my tongue shall sing of your righteousness,
        O / God of mÿ salvátion.

16   O/pen my lips, O Lord, *
        and my mouth / shall procläim ÿöur praise.

17   Had you desired it, I would have / offered sácrifice, *
        but you take no de/light in bürnt-öfferings.

18   The sacrifice of God is a / troubled spírit; *
        a broken and contrite heart, O / God, you will nót despise.

19   Be favorable and gra/cious to Źion, *
        and rebuild the / walls of Jërúsälem.

20   Then you will be pleased with the appointed sacrifices,
        with burnt-offerings / and oblátions; *
        then shall they offer young bul/locks upön your áltar.

If people are holding individual candles, they should be extinguished at this time. The Officiant says the following Collect without chant, and without the usual conclusion.

Almighty God, we pray you graciously to behold this your family, for whom our Lord Jesus Christ was willing to be betrayed, and given into the hands of sinners, and to suffer death upon the cross.

Nothing further is said; but a noise is made, and the burning Christ candle is brought from its hiding place and replaced on the stand.

By its light the ministers and people depart in silence.